A

VOLUNTEER
YOUTH WORKER'S

GUIDE TO UNDERSTANDING
TODAY'S TEENAGERS

A

VOLUNTEER
YOUTH WORKER'S

GUIDE TO UNDERSTANDING
TODAY'S TEENAGERS

MARK OESTREICHER

bare
foot
MINISTRIES

ISBN 978-0-8341-5128-4

Printed in the United States of America

Editor: Audra C. Marvin
Cover Design: Nathan Johnson
Interior Design: Sharon Page

Library of Congress Cataloging-in-Publication Data: 2013908403

10 9 8 7 6 5 4 3 2 1

CONTENTS

INTRODUCTION

A visiting alien (the kind from another planet, that is, not just a foreigner) could watch a bunch of TV shows and movies with teenagers in them and form a fairly robust understanding of the values, thought processes, and inner life of a modern-day teenager.

But the alien would be wrong. Sure, he'd get a few things right. But the two-dimensional sources would primarily mislead. Those flat personifications of teenagers would not provide understanding for these real-life scenarios:

Tyler has loving parents and a great church youth group. He's smart and goes to a great school. In rare instances, Tyler can be hilarious and social. But most of the time, Tyler keeps to himself, brooding and sullen. He seems to be naturally attracted to dark, violent music. He regularly sits in his room, staring at the wall, doing nothing. Why?

Jenna is a creative and social sixteen-year-old who, despite what people might assume about her, has never been a big partier and is fairly inexperienced with alcohol. She is also on her church's youth ministry worship team, deeply connected to her family, and excited about the responsible young adult she is becoming. So why does Jenna break into an unopened bottle of vodka her parents have in the pantry? Why does Jenna, realizing she's going to get caught but wanting to have a bit more, bring vodka to school in a travel mug? And why is she surprised when she gets caught and suspended from school?

Crystal does not fit the easy and obvious stereotypes of a high-school dropout. And she hasn't dropped out yet, but she's secretly working toward it. Crystal has attended an expensive private school for eleven grades, and both of her parents are extremely involved in the school. They have a comfortable home and give Crystal lots of (but not too much) freedom. She has done well enough in school and doesn't seem overly stressed. So why is Crystal secretly taking GED tests, one at a time, so she can drop out of school one semester before graduation? Why is she planning on moving to a farm in another state?

Jason's home is complicated. He has an older brother with learning disabilities who takes most of the family's attention. His parents are present and trying, but they're really odd and quirky. And they struggle financially, living in a rough neighborhood where Jason is a minority. But Jason is about the sharpest, most alive teenager you would ever meet. He's generous and humble, loyal and passionate. Where did that come from? Who should get the credit?

Real, three-dimensional teenagers are complicated. I suppose it's fair to say all humans are. But we adults are not teenagers, and our assumptions about what drives thought and behavior are colored by our adult perspectives and experiences. Add to that the reality that understanding teenagers is a constantly morphing and shape-shifting body of information. Today's teenagers are not the same as teenagers in 1982 (and certainly not the same as teenagers in 1952). Sure, some things haven't changed. But I think it's fair to say that more has changed than has stayed the same.

So our own experiences of being teenagers, if we can remember them at all, are only nominally helpful. If we want to be effective in coming alongside teenagers, helping them develop a real and active, sustainable faith, the ultimate starting point is nurturing your own connections with Jesus. But that's not what this book is about.

If we want to be effective in coming alongside teenagers, helping them develop a real and active, sustainable faith, the second most important piece of the picture is presence; a willingness to be there. But that's not what this book is about either.

So let's go with the third most important thing, which is what this book is about. That thing, the third most important aspect of effective engagement with teenagers, is understanding them.

Sure, there are great examples of fairly clueless youth workers of all ages who have been used by God in the lives of teenagers despite their lack of understanding. But a deep and growing understanding of teenagers and their world will have an impact (a positive one!) on every aspect of what you do in youth ministry, from conversations to small group leadership, from teaching topics to teaching approaches, from event planning to parent interactions, from expectations to the values of your ministry.

That's what I'm hoping to provide you in this short book. It won't be comprehensive, of course. I've studied all this stuff continually, for years, and I'm still learning all the time. I still have blind spots in my understanding. Plus, teenagers and youth culture continue to shift and change.

But I hope to give you a leg up, a cursory overview of the lives and world of the real-life teenagers God has called you to. If you add this knowledge to the first two priorities (your own growing connection with Jesus and your willingness to be present to teenagers), you'll be a better youth worker than most.

NATURE AND NURTURE

Anyone who sets out to describe something about people—educators, psychologists, physicians, anthropologists, journalists, or even comedians—knowingly or unknowingly falls primarily into one of two camps: nature or nurture. Descriptions, of people groups or individuals or behaviors or symptoms, are rooted in the two primary forces that shape those descriptions.

Some of those descriptions (and all the assumptions that go with them) work from or reflect an understanding of nature. Nature merely refers to that which is natural; in this case, physiological realities. From a Christian perspective, we can call this design, since we believe that God intentionally created humans.

When we talk about teenagers from a design point of view, we're referring to those realities that are intrinsic to who they are. These are internal forces that shape who teenagers are. While this is an overstatement, we're primarily referring to body and mind stuff. This is the stuff of objectivity, the observable and quantifiable.

Nurture, however, is the sum total of external forces: influence of family and friends, culture, media, and everything else outside the teenager that has a shaping impact.

These two shaping realities—nature and nurture—are often debated as to which is dominant. I'm not going to add to that debate. Instead, I'm going to work with an assumption I think you'll easily agree with: Both have an enormous shaping influence on the lives of real teenagers.

Take the examples of the teenagers above, for example. Did Jenna make the stupid choice of bringing vodka to school because it's in her nature to do so? Likely not; but we do know that teenagers have underdeveloped brains and that the most underdeveloped part of their brains is the part responsible for wisdom, impulse control, and decision making. So, yeah, there's probably a nature factor playing into that. But wouldn't there also have to be some external shaping forces in her decision? Otherwise, where would she have come up with the idea that this might be a cool thing? Or a fun thing? Even the presence of the vodka bottle in her home is an external shaping reality.

Tyler is dark and moody. Is that because all teenagers, or at least teenage boys, are physiologically predisposed to moodiness? The first framing voice of adolescence, a guy named Stanley Hall, would have said that was the case. But surely, we know that there are external pressures adding to Tyler's mindset. In fact, while Tyler's disposition is common in the U.S., he'd be a rare teenager in most other cultures around the world.

The same dissection could be done with our other two examples (Crystal and Jason).

So that's the course we're going to chart here. We're going to start with the internal stuff—the physiological stuff; then we'll circle back around and look at the external stuff—the cultural realities.

NATURE, BY DESIGN

Now that you have a basic understanding of nature, I'm going to back pedal just a bit. Sorry. I have to toss out this minor caveat, this little wrench in the works: Much of what I'm going to describe in the following pages about the physiological realities of teenagers might still have nurture realities to it.

Here's an example: We've recently learned a bunch of wild new stuff about the adolescent brain, thanks to the invention of the MRI, which allows for real-time scans of healthy teenage brains. That's how we learned about that underdeveloped aspect of their brains—the decision-making part. But what we don't know is whether teenage brains were always this way or if they've become this way due to external forces and expectations (or lack of expectations!). So I can't tell you that all of what I'm going to describe is absolutely and unequivocally part of God's design. Maybe it is, maybe it isn't. But most of what I'll describe certainly seems fair to ascribe to design.

THE TURBULENT TEENS

I remember a news story I read not too long ago that was wild. It was about a new island being discovered. Now, a few hundred years ago, that wouldn't have been a big deal; adventurers discovered new geography all the time. But these days, we seem to have a pretty solid lock on what land exists and what land doesn't exist. So a new island is kind of a big deal.

But the truth wasn't that the island had always been there and was suddenly seen. It was actually a new island, created due to some seismic shifts combined with a small drop in the water level of the ocean. What was previously just below the water level was now just above the water level. Land, ho!

This new island felt metaphorical to me. It reminded me of teenagers (no, not just of a zit appearing on an otherwise calm, adolescent face). It reminded me that the earth is growing and changing. It's organic (mostly). It's part of a big ecosystem with all kinds of forces pushing in all directions. That, my youth worker friend, is very much what's going on in the mind and body of every teenager you'll ever meet.

IF THERE'S ONE THING WE KNOW ABOUT ADOLESCENT DEVELOPMENT, IT'S THAT EVERYTHING IS CHANGING.

You know how people refer to that wild and volatile period of development from about two to three years old as the terrible twos? Well, I think of the years from puberty to young adulthood as the turbulent teens. I say this because, if there's one thing we know about adolescent development, it's that everything is changing. In fact, there's not another period of the human lifespan, other than the first two years of life, with so much change. Adolescence is almost synonymous with change.

Their bodies are changing. Their minds are changing. Their friendships are (often) changing. Their emotions are changing. Their sense of independence is changing. Their faith (whatever faith it is) is changing. Sure, they're growing. But growing implies more of the same. And the changes of adolescence are certainly not more of the same. These are substantive changes; changes in quality, not just quantity.

This has massive implications for us as youth workers. Every teenager, at various points through the adolescent journey of change, feels abnormal. Every teenager is disoriented by the sheer volume of change. Every teenager feels a bit lost at points. Every teenager feels like a freak. One of the most important ministries we can have, armed with our awareness and presence, is to normalize their experience. This isn't about downplaying or dismissing the tumult they feel. Normalizing doesn't mean saying, "You're not so unique; get over yourself."

Normalizing means to come alongside teenagers and help them feel okay about themselves. Help them see that the changes they're going through are all part of God's great love for them. Point them to John 10:10, where Jesus says, "I have come to give you life, and life to the full." And tell them that Jesus loves them so much that he wants them to have full and meaningful and passionate lives; but, in order to experience that fullness of life, their brains and bodies have to morph from the limits of childhood. Acknowledge that it's normal to feel abnormal. It's common to feel uncommon. It would be peculiar not to feel peculiar.

And tell them they'll be okay. Live this out by staying present, by not being shocked or disgusted, by incarnating God's unconditional love and acceptance. Say and live,

"You're awesome, and I'm going to show you how awesome you are by sticking with you."

TRANSFORMERS

As I write this, the third *Transformers* movie is in the theaters. Since it is clearly a cash magnet, I expect there will be another twenty or so sequels in this franchise. Sure, it's all computer-generated graphics; but when those cars and trucks crank and turn and shape-shift in midair, landing again as giant mechanical warriors, it looks pretty awesome.

The process in teenagers is a bit slower and seemingly less awesome. But when you compare a ten-year-old to an eighteen-year-old and stop to think about the transformation the body goes through in those few years, well, it's more awesome (and it's not computer generated!).

I've spent my adult life working with middle schoolers, so I really get a close-up view of this change. I recently said goodbye to a small group of eighth-grade young men heading into my church's high school ministry.

They came to me, fewer than three short years ago, as incoming sixth graders. Every one of them was shorter than me. They were boys. They were shaped like boys, sounded like boys, and often smelled like boys. Today, all but one of them is taller than me. Most of them have voices that have dropped a good octave or two. They still smell, but at least they know how to mask it now. They really are young men.

I had a previous small group of middle school guys who are now headed into their senior year of high school. And holy cow—they make my recent batch of guys look, once again, like boys by comparison.

The physical changes that occur in the five to eight years following puberty are, in my opinion, some of God's most amazing work. Yeah, there's some other pretty amazing stuff about the human body. But the substantive, qualitative change that takes place in the bodies of teenagers is nothing short of mind-blowing.

It's the obvious change. So it's probably the change you're most familiar with.

Clothes fit for mere months as both height and shape continually shift. Voices change (in girls too, by the way). Hair starts growing in places they never knew they would have it. Breasts grow on girls, and guys' penises and testicles grow in both size and function. Sweat increases. Muscles increase.

Let's stop there, to remind you of something I already told you. Every teenager, at one point or many points or all points, believes he or she is growing wrong. They might think they're too short. Too tall. Too big around. Not big around enough. Behind in breast development or too advanced in breast development or lopsided in breast development. Not hairy enough in their pubic areas or underarms. Too hairy.

AS YOUTH WORKERS, WE HAVE TO BE SO CAREFUL ABOUT WHAT WE DO AND DON'T SAY ABOUT THE PHYSICAL CHANGES UNFOLDING BEFORE OUR EYES.

As youth workers, we have to be so careful about what we do and don't say about the physical changes unfolding before our eyes. Acknowledging growth and physical changes (well, some of them) can be a good and affirming thing. But not always, since some teenagers are extremely self-conscious. And acknowledging, for example, that Dude A has grown a ton in front of Dude B, who hasn't grown a ton, can be hurtful to Dude B.

A good rule of thumb is to positively (and appropriately) comment on how cool it is to see a teenager becoming a young adult but not to focus on particular aspects of that change. At the same time, we have to open up these conversations in small groups, inviting students into a safe place of talking about the changes going on in their bodies. And, pepper your teaching time and other talking-to-everyone moments with normalizing comments like, "Everyone feels abnormal at times, but you're going to turn out just fine," and, "Remember that how you look isn't who you are."

BRAINIACS

I think the changes going on in the teenage brain are the most significant changes of adolescence and the most important for every youth worker to understand. All the other changes we experience (and they experience even more!) flow out of the cognitive changes transforming their brains.

Let's start with this: During the two years leading up to puberty, the brain goes into an unprecedented growth mode in one particular area. Neurons are the wiring of the brain, the microscopic switches that conduct energy, moving information around the brain and allowing it to think or react or remember. Grouped together, neurons are referred to as neural pathways. Think of them as the highways of the mind. In those two pre-pubescent years, the brain grows millions of new neurons, millions more than are needed, or will even be present, in adulthood. At puberty, a toggle switch gets tripped, and the process reverses itself. In the years following puberty, millions of neurons are winnowed back, literally disappearing.

But the fascinating thing about this process is how the winnowing takes place. Brain researchers have discovered that those neurons that get to stay and play are those that get used. And neurons that don't get used are laid off, fired for lack of function or performance. It's corporate "right-sizing" on a cerebral playing field.

Jay Giedd, chief of brain imaging in the child psychiatry branch at the National Institute of Mental Health, calls it a use-it-or-lose-it principle. He even says that teenage brains get hard wired for life and form the basics of how they will process information for the remainder of their lifespan.

This has implications for us! We are called to be stewards of adolescent brain development, understanding that how we help students use their brains will have implications for how they use their brains for the rest of their lives. With that reality in play, would it be better to cram them full of information in the hope that they can regurgitate it, or to help them be thoughtful, considering things, growing in wisdom, asking good questions, and contemplating faith? (Clearly, I think the latter is better.)

There's another huge shift taking place in teenage brains, begun at puberty, and it's the awakening of abstract thinking. The human brain goes through a whole series of developmental stages in how it processes information. But the last of those shifts, like moving from fourth gear to fifth on an open highway, is the move from concrete thinking to abstract thinking.

ABSTRACT THINKING IS THE *ABILITY* TO THINK ABOUT THINKING.

Children and preteens are limited in their thinking. Their brains are only able to perceive and think about concrete, defined realities. The slow and gradual opening of abstract thought changes everything. In short, abstract thinking is the *ability to think about thinking.* But it's more than that.

Abstract thinking allows for speculation. It allows for third-person perspectives (I can now see myself from another's perspective). It allows for paradox. It creates space for empathy (which requires a third-person perspective and a feeling of what that other person might be experiencing). And—this is a biggie—they can think about abstract faith ideas, which, honestly, includes all faith ideas.

Consider an example: You're talking in your small group, filled with middle schoolers, about an abstract spiritual topic like following Jesus. Let's face it; that's abstract language because we're not actually talking about literally walking behind a physical person named Jesus. Because moving into the use of abstract thinking is gradual, you'll have a variety of perspectives present about what following Jesus actually means. Some will be limited to concrete thinking and literal terms. They'll picture, in their minds, the physical movement of walking behind Jesus but will have a fuzzy sense that you mean something more than that (particularly if they've been around church long enough to hear this kind of metaphorical language before). Others will be able to conceptualize that you're talking about conforming our lives to be more like Jesus (even though they would never use that description).

Here's one of the major challenges of youth ministry: You have no idea, at any given moment, who's thinking abstractly and who's thinking concretely. If they respond, you can often tell. But if they're all just sitting there thinking, you're in the dark. That's why it's so important to ask a ton of questions, checking for understanding, asking students to reveal what they're hearing and thinking.

Abstract thinking isn't a muscle, but I like to think of it that way. It's a helpful metaphor. If it were a muscle, it would be a brand-new, right-out-of-the-box, puberty gift from God. But it's a muscle that hasn't been used, and it's super flabby and lacking any strength whatsoever. It has to be used and exercised in order to get strong.

Get this: When we help students use their abstract thinking, we're helping them develop the capacity for spiritual growth. Spiritual growth is much more than being able to think well, of course. But developing an owned, adult faith requires abstract thinking.

So ask lots of speculation questions. Check for understanding. Use concrete illustrations, examples, and object lessons to bridge the gap from concrete to abstract. Allow for disorientation and confusion, but stay with it. Celebrate good, hard questions, and don't give easy answers.

I LOVE YOU! I HATE YOU!

Let's say you're a girls' small group leader (guys, feel free to transpose this story!). There's one particularly bubbly and talkative girl who seems to really like being around you. In fact, she regularly tells you what an awesome leader you are and how cool she thinks you are. But then, seemingly out the blue, she switches opinions.

Suddenly, she's avoiding you. And you overhear her telling one of the other girls that you're totally lame. The next week, she's back to singing your praises again.

If this sort of emotional roller coaster feels whiplashy to you, imagine what it feels like to the girl! Certainly, there might be circumstantial reasons for the emotional switch you experience with this girl; and you should certainly check to see if you've hurt her feelings or done something else. But the reality is that teenagers—particularly young and middle teens—are going through a massive upheaval of emotions, and it is foreign terrain to them.

Have you ever moved to a new city? It takes a while to get used to things—where they are and how they work. For a while, everything is a bit disorienting. The same holds true for teenagers and their emotions because emotions are abstract!

So, with the onset of abstract thinking, teenagers move from a limited selection of fairly concrete emotions to a massive selection of highly nuanced emotions. But their lack of familiarity with these emotions and their limited ability to understand them causes a significant amount of disorientation. In fact, one of the other brain development discoveries of the last decade is that teenagers' temporal lobes (just behind the temples on the sides of your head) are underdeveloped. The temporal lobes are, among other things, responsible for emotional understanding and inter-pretation. By the way, boys' temporal lobes are even more underdeveloped than girls', which says something about why boys struggle with emotions even more than girls.

I had an experience with my daughter when she was about thirteen or fourteen that illustrates this shift well. Liesl and I were having dinner together at home, just the two of us. Casually, without any emotion, I asked her what homework she had that evening. And she went ballistic.

With a raised voice and an accusatory face, she yelled, "Why are you always yelling at me about my homework!?"

In shock, I responded, still not yelling, "I wasn't yelling, Liesl; I was just asking about your homework."

"You were yelling; you're always yelling at me!"

At this point, my buttons were starting to get pushed, and I could tell this conversation trajectory was going nowhere helpful, quickly. I took a breath and told her she needed to go up to her bedroom, and when she was ready to talk about this without yelling at me, she could come back down.

Liesl stomped up to her bedroom and slammed the door. Not three minutes passed before I heard her door open, and I heard her coming down the stairs, quietly crying.

"Daddy, I'm so sorry. I don't know why I freaked out like that." (sniff, sniff)

I saw a possible opportunity to normalize her experience. I asked, "Could I try to explain what I think is happening?" With her agreement, I asked, "Do you ever feel sad or depressed, and don't know why?"

Quietly, through sniffs, she responded, "Yeah."

I asked, "Do you ever feel tons of energy and excitement but don't know why?"

She perked up: "Yeah, Emily and I got in trouble in school today because we were so giggly, and there wasn't any reason for it!"

I explained to Liesl how kids' brains and teenage brains aren't the same and that her brain is changing to allow her to think in new ways. I explained that her brain changes gave her the opportunity to experience all kinds of new emotions. I told her what Jesus promises, in John 10:10, about his coming to give us a full life, and how, in God's great love for her, he wants her to have a life full of rich emotions. I told her that the transition into new, adult emotions could feel awkward and confusing at times but that she'd get used to them, and it would be good.

WE LIKE THE SAME THINGS!

The cognitive shift taking place in the brains of teenagers impacts their friendships also. The short, oversimplified explanation of this could be summed up thus:

- Childhood friendships are normally formed based on proximity: You and I are friends because we live near each other or spend a lot of time in the same place.
- Teenager friendships (and adult friendships) are normally based on affinity: You and I are friends because we like the same things.

The primary reason for this is that teenagers, with their brand-new thinking ability, start to become more (big word alert!) *differentiated*. As they set off in search of an identity, struggling with the *Who am I?* question, and start to perceive themselves from others' perspectives, they naturally want to form friendships with those who share the same interests (even though many teenagers haven't settled on what their interests are, at least not for the long run).

Put a group of seven-year-olds in a room with a tub of Legos, and while there might be a bully or a natural social order that begins to form, they'll quickly find their way. That's because they're just not that different from each other, and they're not aware of the differences that do exist. Put a group of sixteen-year-olds in a room, and they're instantly testing and politicking, watching for cues as to whom they should align with or avoid. It's like the first episode of every season of Survivor: "Whom should I form an alliance with?"

This shift, like all the others, can be exciting or harrowing, full of possibility or full of pain. Think of it this way: Lucas and Aaron have been best friends since childhood; but now, Lucas and Aaron are becoming very different from each other. Lucas knows that other kids think his friend is weird. Lucas also knows that if he hangs out with Aaron, other kids will label him weird too. Lucas's mom pressures him to hang out with Aaron, but he doesn't want to because it's too socially risky; and ultimately, Lucas feels like he doesn't have anything in common with Aaron anymore.

I find that teenage friendships (particularly young and middle teens; older teens start to become a bit more comfortable with who they are, and these generalizations apply less) tend to follow predictable patterns.

Girls, whose friendships require a high level of loyalty, vulnerability, and shared emotional experience, tend to form friendships of two or three. The high degree of commitment and investment, combined with fragile self-images and gossip, normally mean that a friendship group of four girls can't sustain itself. Either the group will split in two, or one girl will be booted (or leave) to join another friendship group.

GIRLS FORM THEIR FRIENDSHIPS BY TALKING, AND GUYS FORM THEIR FRIENDSHIPS BY DOING THINGS.

Girls form their friendships on emotional engagement. Guys, not so much. Guys form their friendships on shared experience. Another way to say this is that girls form their friendships by talking, and guys form their friendships by doing things.

Guy friendships tend to fall into one of two extremes. Either they run in an affinity group based on shared interest—a mini culture with its own norms, behaviors, styles, power structure, language, and preferences, or they are loners. I have noticed a trend in the last couple decades of more and more teenage guys who do not have any significant friendships. They might have someone they consider a friend because they got together once to play video games, but there is a shocking amount of teenage guys who have no idea how to get or be a friend. As youth workers, we need to be intentional about providing contexts and encouragement to these guys, helping them form friendships where they're known and belong.

UPGRADING THE SPIRITUAL OS

The operating system of your computer runs in the background, creating a context for all the programs you run. The OS is the playground, and the programs are the individual pieces of equipment—slides and monkey bars and seesaws. Every so often, new versions of operating systems are released, and over time, we all upgrade. Theoretically, the upgraded OS allows for all kinds of cool new things; and, if programs are upgraded to work with the new OS, they improve in speed, complexity, and performance.

This is a perfect metaphor for what's going on in the spiritual development of teenagers, from a developmental perspective. The onset of abstract thinking is a brain operating system upgrade. And it allows for the programs of spiritual understanding and growth to be upgraded as well in speed, complexity, and performance.

Pretty much every teenager's faith gets an overhaul during adolescence, whatever that faith might be, and however articulated or unarticulated it might be.

A case study might flesh this out a bit:

Tanya grew up in church and had a healthy childhood understanding of her faith. Tanya walks through life with a metaphorical backpack of faith. It's always with her; it's her faith and worldview all rolled into one. You might think of it as Tanya's systematic theology, in that it's her cobbled-together understanding of how spiritual things work and her place and role in the whole thing. The faith bits that make up this constellation of belief include a wide variety of interconnected parts, some tested and deeply held, others inherited from her family or church, and others absorbed from marketing and peer messages or her experience of life.

Let's say one of Tanya's faith bits is a composite belief that:

1. God is in control.
2. God is loving and good.
3. Good things happen to good people.

(You can see that some of this is accurate and theologically sound, while the third bit is more of a cultural presumption than a sound piece of biblical truth.)

Tanya cruises through life, and this particular set of beliefs works just fine for her. But one day, a massive natural disaster plays out in a country on the other side of the world. Thousands of innocent people die, and the human tragedy and suffering are staggering. The story plays out on the news and in discussions at school, and Tanya is momentarily consumed by it.

This causes Tanya's set of beliefs to be pulled out of her backpack of faith and examined. For young teens and middle teens, this usually happens at a somewhat subconscious level; but for older teens, the process of belief examination can be very conscious (really, the level of conscious or subconscious examination is mostly dependent on two things: teens' experiences with abstract thinking, and adults who enter into discussion with them about these issues).

However it goes down, Tanya realizes that her belief no longer works for her. Either God isn't in control, or God isn't loving or good, or bad things happen to good people, or some combination of all three.

Tanya has three choices at this point:

1. Tanya can say (again, consciously or subconsciously), "Well, that sure doesn't seem true, so I guess I don't believe it anymore." This rejection of childhood beliefs in the face of contrary evidence is super common for teenagers. It's one of the primary reasons that teenagers move away from the faith that was at one time real and important to them.

2. Tanya can also respond with, "What I believed doesn't seem true, but it's all I have, so I guess I'll just believe it anyway." Tanya shoves the faith bits back into her backpack of faith and continues holding to her childhood (now childish) beliefs. This is one of the primary reasons most of our churches are full of adults who live by a semi-Christian moral code but not an active faith that informs their daily living, not a thriving and vibrant faith. And why should it be thriving or active? An eight-year-old's faith system shouldn't be sustainable for an adult.

3. Tanya's third option is the most difficult and often requires the help of an engaged adult: She can upgrade the beliefs—through conversation, reflection, Scripture, other reading, or the work of the Holy Spirit—to a more complex and nuanced, adult-like understanding of truth.

See, like it or not, all the spiritual stuff we talk about in youth ministry is abstract, at least to some degree. And, because speculation—a major component of faith development—is an abstract thinking function and not something teenagers are competent or comfortable with, it's critical that we youth workers constantly host speculation. Ask lots of *what if* and *why* questions. Walk alongside teenagers in their questions. Never guilt them for having doubts, but use those as an opportunity for healthy and necessary spiritual conversations.

NATURE:
SHAPED BY WIND AND WATER

Have you ever been to, or at least seen photos of, those amazing canyons that have been shaped over years by wind and water? The shaping, of course, takes place in little insignificant bits, over time.

Of course, some teenagers have had catastrophic events in their lives—like an earthquake or another massive force of nature—that have indelibly shaped them in a single moment. But all of them are molded and pressed and chiseled, over time, by a variety of external forces.

For good or ill, parents are a primary shaping force, of course. But so is the world around them, the culture they live in. Think of it this way: Take a baby and then feed her a steady diet, over the span of sixteen years, with a constant bombardment of messages (visual, print, lyrical, peer) that tell her . . .

- Looking good and sexy will make you more attractive to others, which will make you happy.
- If you're not one of the beautiful people, mask yourself to get as close as you can.
- You are a consumer, and who you are is primarily defined by what you own and consume.
- Be yourself, to a degree; but if being yourself causes you to be less approved by others, accommodate their wishes.

I'm sure you can see how it would be almost impossible for those messages not to shape her in some ways, unless there are consistent and compelling counter messages being delivered from trusted sources.

So, if we're going to fully understand teenagers (remember: We want to increase our understanding of teenagers because it's the third most important thing we can do to increase our effectiveness as youth workers), we have to be students of the cultural forces that shape them.

Surely, we could explore this for thousands of pages. But we don't have space for that here. So I'm going to unpack four specific shaping forces in youth culture. I've chosen these four specifically because they're both less obvious than some of the more overt messages listed in the example of the sixteen-year-old girl above and because they're newer cultural realities (and you might not be aware of them).

SPLINTERED YOUTH CULTURE

As I wrote earlier, the idea of adolescence as a distinct, quantifiable life stage is only about a hundred years old. But even younger is the concept of youth culture, which really sprang onto the scene after World War II, particularly with the then-new holding pens of mandatory high school.

During the sixtyish years of modern youth culture, the fabric and feel have shifted many times. A significant metamorphosis took place sometime around the turn of the millennium. This substantive shift occurred because of a surprising reality: Youth culture had become the dominant culture in America. While this was a gradual (but still fast) process, and there's probably not a single marker or cause, the reality is that prior to the late '90s, youth culture was always a subculture. But, as young Baby Boomers and older Gen-Xers started to have children, those parents refused to give up many of the cultural trappings of adolescence.

Let me give you this example from my own life. I'm forty-eight as I write this; I was born in 1963 and graduated from high school in 1981. Growing up, the only music I shared with my parents was our Firestone Christmas album, which made its way onto the family turntable for a few weeks each December. Otherwise, the musical preferences of my parents were completely different from my own.

Fast forward: My two teenage children (seventeen and thirteen as I write this) and I share about an 80–90% overlap in our musical preferences. We regularly split the cost of downloading albums we both (or all) want. We never fight over the radio dial in the car. I never find myself saying or thinking, *What in the world are you listening to? It sounds like cats fighting!*

Another example: My youth pastor friend Danny accompanied the local middle school's eighth grade on a class trip from San Diego to Washington, DC. Danny and the class teacher were the only male chaperons; there were four or five moms who also chaperoned the trip.

During the middle of the trip, I was exchanging text messages with Danny about something or other, and I asked how the trip was going. He responded, *If I see one more mom-thong, I think I'm going to scream.*

Let's face it; the generation gap is a cultural relic. It's gone, at least between teenagers and the one or two generations preceding them. In many ways, there's more of a generation gap between older adults and middle-aged adults than there is between teenagers and their parents.

But youth culture—if we can personify it for a moment—doesn't want to be the dominant culture. Youth culture has embedded into its DNA a desire (really, a developmental need) to be other, to differentiate itself from the culture at large. As a result of this tension (and other factors), youth culture went through a shocking change in the late '90s and early 2000s: It splintered and went underground.

Sure, there's that dominant youth culture; but that's pop culture. That dominant youth culture is the stuff of music and movies and TV and clothing styles and slang, most of which are identified and elevated by adults trying to market to teenagers and adolescent-obsessed adults.

But the place where real teenagers live is splintered into thousands of unique cultures, each with their own preferences, language, styles, behavioral norms, and power structures.

In the 1960s and 1970s—even in the 1980s—youth workers were told that, to reach a high school campus, they only needed to reach the key influencers. Those were, in most schools, assumed to be the football team captains and the cheerleading captains. From there, the entire relational power structure of the school trickled down. That structure is gone.

Here's a wild statement: *Every youth group is a multicultural youth group, whether it's got racial and economic diversity or not.* Unless you have a youth group of three kids who are all homeschooled, you have a multicultural youth group because the students in your group are all living (particularly in their non-youth-group lives) in different cultures.

This reality is both a challenge and an opportunity.

BELONGING GOGGLES

———

Belonging predates creation. That seems wild, doesn't it? But think about it: God has eternally existed in the relationality of the Trinity, an interdependent relationship of belonging. So, when God created you and me in his own image, one of the characteristics he put in us is a need for belonging. Our desire for belonging is an indicator of our made-in-the-image-of-God-ness. It's a beautiful and wonderful thing.

But teenagers today have a super-amplified need for belonging. And it's because of the splintering of youth culture that we just talked about. When youth culture splintered, it was like the relational tide rushing out, creating an enormous pull behind it. That pull is the almost desperate need to find a place to belong.

Another way to imagine this shift: Back in the '50s and '60s, the average teenager was going through life wearing a pair of identity goggles (using imaginary language here!). Identity—*Who am I?*—was the dominant need of most teenagers (it's still one of the most significant aspects of being a teenager, btw). As teenagers walked through life, everything else they looked at, both literally and figuratively, was colored by the tint of their identity goggles. This included their search for where they belonged. *Where do I belong?* was filtered by *Who am I?*

But now that there's no longer one monolithic youth culture, now that youth culture has splintered, teenagers are left nervously looking left and right, high and low, in a winner-takes-all, loser-takes-nothing grasp at belonging. The average teenager today is, as a result, wearing belonging goggles.

That desperate search for belonging colors everything. Now, *Who am I?* is filtered through *Where do I belong?* That's a huge change and should have big implications on our approaches to youth ministry.

For instance, belonging has always been an important aspect of youth ministry. But today's teenager isn't even willing to consider your beliefs or teaching ideas if you aren't willing to offer her unconditional belonging first. Unless he experiences belonging (and chooses to participate in it), he won't try on your behaviors.

Our youth groups have to have belonging as a core DNA component, a central practice, a value that trumps other values. And, when we stop to think about it, we get to host students into the best place of belonging ever: You belong to Christ and to the body of Christ.

BOY (OR GIRL) IN THE BUBBLE

Another factor dramatically shaping today's teenagers has been a gradual shift over the last several decades. It's been so gentle and subtle, in fact, that you might not even be aware that anything has changed.

This shift is the gradual move to an experience of the world where teenagers only and exclusively interact with peers. They live in a homogeneous world, at least in terms of life stage. Gone are the days when teenagers apprenticed next to adults, in the world of adults. Gone are the days when teenagers were responsible for providing care for the younger children in the family (of course, there are exceptions).

Now, don't get me wrong: I'm not one of those nostalgic guys who longs for everything to go back to the way things used to be. No question about it, being fifteen years old in 1850 had its challenges that no longer exist. So, yeah, that's not my point.

But think of the average day of an average sixteen-year-old:

6:00 a.m.: Wake up and get ready for school. No meaningful connection with anyone. Shoot a few texts to friends and check Facebook. You don't even see your dad, and you only exchange a sentence or two about logistics with your mom.

7:30 a.m.: High school! For the next seven hours (give or take), you're kept in a very large holding pen. The only adults in there with you are those who (whatever their motives) are paid to be there. Even if they have fantastic motives, they're still coming into your world, not the other way around.

3:00 p.m.: You either head to sports practice (more peers, more adults who are paid to be with you; and even if they're volunteers, they're still coming into your world), or you head to your afterschool job. Your supervisor is a twenty-two-year old who's seriously stuck in the early stages of extended adolescence. Even though there's a minimal amount of responsibility in this job, you're mostly doing a starter, repetitive function (like punching numbers on a cash register). If you don't have an afterschool job or sports practice, you either hang out with friends, or you head home to start on homework (in isolation).

6:00 p.m.: You might have dinner with your family but not if you're average. The average teenager spends a grand total of fifteen minutes a week with his or her dad, and only five of those are without a TV on.

7:30 p.m.: You withdraw to your bedroom to work on homework or partner with a peer on the same. You might have a job (see 3:00 p.m.). Or you might go to youth group, where, just like school, you spend all your time in a homogeneous world of teenagers, where the only adults are those who are paid to be there or volunteer to enter into the world of teenagers.

Here's the dealio: Today's teenagers live in almost complete isolation from the world of adults. They have no idea, really, what it means to be an adult because they never have the opportunity to observe adults being adults in the world of adults. The on ramps to adulthood have been removed.

HI, I'M A 27-YEAR-OLD TEENAGER

Sure, a twenty-seven-year-old isn't technically a teenager. But the average twenty-seven-year-old is just barely reaching the waning years of an extended adolescence that stretches, say researchers, to about thirty years old for most.

Seriously, this redefines everything, right? (Hey, an advantage to me, as a forty-eight-year-old, is that I get to stay middle aged for a whole lot longer!)

Think back to the last section for a minute (how teenagers live in a world of isolation, separated from the world of adults). Can you see how one of the results of this would be teenagers continuing in an extended form of the teenage world? How could we expect them to do anything else? We've removed the on ramps to adulthood, we don't give them meaningful responsibility and expectation (absolutely essential to transitioning to adulthood), and we treat them like children throughout their teenage years and often into their young twenties (the fancy word for this, by the way, is *infantilization*).

Adolescence is so long now that researchers talk about it in three distinct phases, each becoming its own developmental life stage, its own field of research and study:

11–14: young teen (or early adolescence)

15–20: late teen (or middle adolescence)

21–30: emerging adulthood

Now, you might be saying, *Marko, hold on. As much as I care about those twenty-somethings and their stuck-ness, they're not my primary calling. I'm called to teenagers, and this doesn't really seem to be about teenagers.*

Can you hear my (extremely masculine) voice ringing out, "Wrong!" in your mind (btw, my voice sounds way more masculine when it's imaginary than it does in real life)?

Think of it this way: We've taken what was an eighteen-month process in the early 1900s and a six-year process in the 1970s, and we've made it an almost twenty-year process. That means that all the stuff going on in the process is extended and protracted and elongated.

While adolescence begins (with puberty) younger and younger all the time, abstract thinking is being postponed. Meaningful responsibility is postponed. Teenagers (and young adults) are, like I wrote in the last section, treated as if they were children for more and more years.

While some adolescent issues are being pushed younger and younger, others are consistently being postponed, not being faced until the late twenties. And that means that the teenagers in your youth group (even if you have nothing to do with the twenty-somethings who likely don't attend your church anyway) are a different breed of teenager than you were at that age.

What would it look like for you to be a countercultural influence on this trend? What would it look like for us to offer meaningful responsibility and expectation in our churches? What would it look like for us to stop treating teenagers like children? What would it look like for us to reintroduce on ramps to adulthood? What would it look like for your church (and your youth ministry) to provide teenagers the opportunity to rub shoulders with adults in the world of adults, not only with adults who come into the world of teenagers?

WRAPPING IT UP

I hope, as you get to the end of this little book, that you've grown in your understanding of teenagers in general. But more than that, I hope you grew in your understanding of real teenagers, not imaginary ones. I hope you thought of names and faces and life stories. I hope your affection for real teenagers increased.

And I pray that your influence in the lives of real teenagers will also grow. I pray you will have more patience, normalize their experiences, help them exercise their speculation muscles, and provide them opportunities to step out of the isolated world they live in.

Our calling, remember, is not to create a teenage island, where fifteen-year-olds can develop an active faith that only works as long as they stay on the island. Our calling is to come alongside teenagers on their journeys to adulthood.

May the grace and peace and power of Christ be with you mightily as you pour out your life in these ways!